MINI MOTORCYCLE BIBLE

TECTUM
PUBLISHERS

MOTORCY
MINI

CLE BIBLE

EXCELSIOR & HENDERSON
MOTORCYCLES · SUPPLIES

EXCELSIOR BICYCLES
AND REPAIRS

SHARPENED
SAWS FILED
ELECTRICALLY
BABY CARRIAGES AND
KIDDIE CARTS RETIRED

© 2010   Tectum Publishers
Godefriduskaai 22
2000 Antwerp
Belgium
info@tectum.be
+ 32 3 226 66 73
www.tectum.be

ISBN: 978-90-79761-42-5
WD: 2010/9021/4
(105)

All Photos supplied by Roland Brown
Photos (c) Roland Brown, by: James Adam Bolton,
Roland Brown, Jack Burnicle, Jason Critchell, Gold &
Goose, Patrick Gosling, Phil Masters, Mac McDiarmid,
Oli Tennent Photos from Roland Brown library/Riders
for Health, by: BMW, Critchell/ Tennent, Double Red,
Gold & Goose, Milagro, Nelson/Riles

except pages 86-89, 126-129, 198-201,
258-269, 274-277, 290-293, 298-301,
366-369 by Reinhard Lintelmann

Design : Gunter Segers

PREFACE

One of the most remarkable things about the development of the motorcycle over more than a century is how little the experience of riding a bike has changed in that time. Of course there are huge differences between today's sophisticated superbikes and the earliest models, let alone the wooden-framed Einspur, or One-track, with which German engineer Gottlieb Daimler began motorcycling's story in 1885. But the motorcycle's essential appeal has changed little since the basic layout of the "iron horse" - with its engine slung low between two wheels, and steering via a pair of handlebars linked to the front wheel - was established early in the last century.

If the experience of leaning into a turn with the wind tugging at your neck remains little changed, the machines themselves and the way they are used have been transformed. During the first half of the last century, most motorbikes were used purely for transport, although there were always enthusiasts who appreciated the style and performance of machines as varied as Brough's Superior and Indian's Chief. Increasingly, though, bikes were seen as a lifestyle statement and a form of entertainment. After British twins had dominated the 1950s and '60s, Honda's four-cylinder CB750 arrived in 1969 to begin the superbike era of ever-increasing performance, in which many machines are used for leisure as much as for transport. Recent years have seen a continuation of this theme, plus an explosion of technology as manufacturers offer a variety of engine types, and a huge range of models from lightweight sports machines to luxury tourers. Many incorporate sophisticated electronics, such as BMW's S1000RR with its anti-lock brakes, alternative engine maps and traction control system. Meanwhile firms including Harley-Davidson have been successful with modern models that recreate the simplicity and styling cues of an earlier age. If the Mini Motorcycle Bible highlights one thing above all, it's the fascinating diversity of bikes over the years.

Roland Brown
MOTORCYCLE JOURNALIST AND PHOTOGRAPHER

Benelli • Italy • 750 Sei • 1975 • roadster

BMW • Germany • R32 • 1925 • roadster

BMW • Germany • R60 • 1969 • roadster

BMW • Germany • R1200 GS • 2004 • dual-purpose

BMW • Germany • F800S • 2006 • roadster

BMW • Germany • S1000RR • 2010 • sports

OIL INJECTION

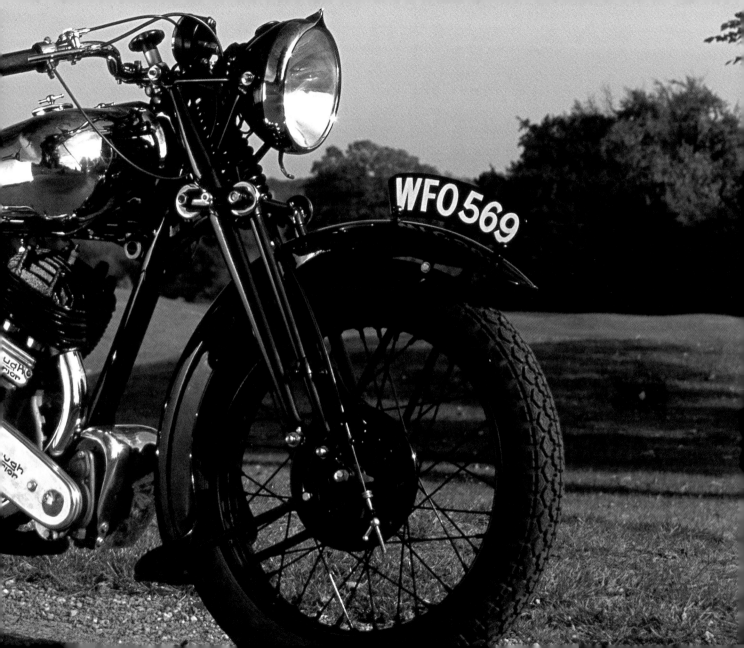

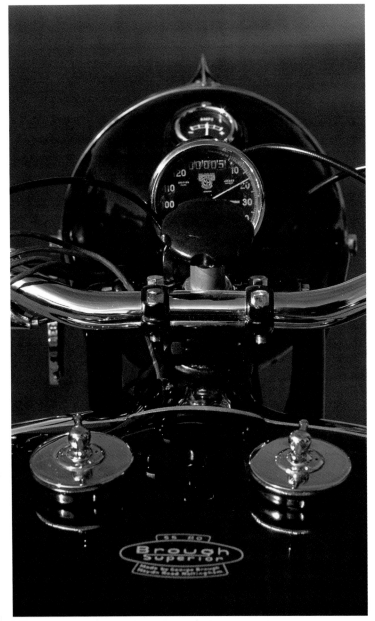

De Dion Bouton • France • 1,75 PS • 1899 • tricycle

Douglas • Britain • 3.5hp twin • 1920 • roadster

SV 5181

Douglas.

Douglas • Britain • Dragonfly • 1955 • roadster

Ducati • Italy • M900 Monster • 1993 • roadster

FN • Belgium • FN Four • 1905 • roadster

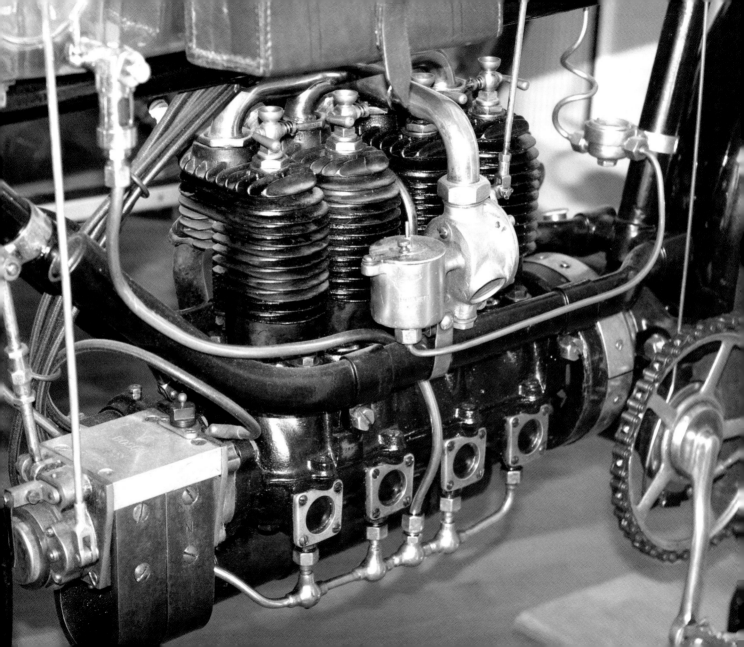

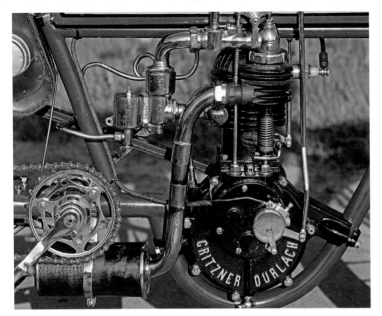

Harley-Davidson • USA • Sportster 1200 • 1989 • roadster

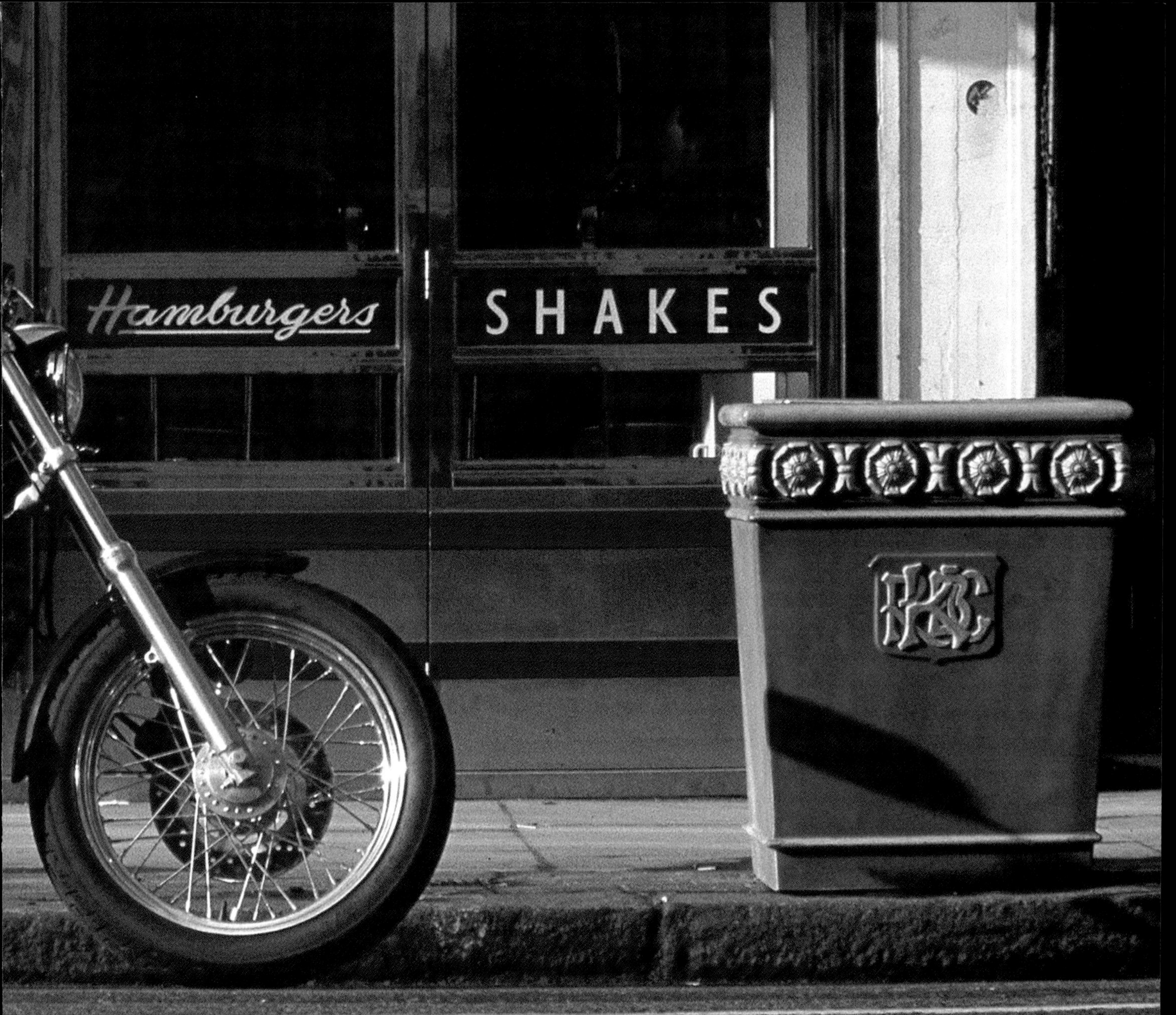
Hamburgers
SHAKES

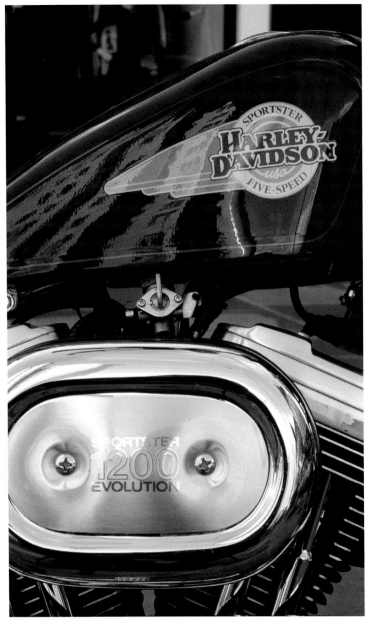

COCKTAILS

Honda • Japan • CB92 • 1961 • sports

Honda • Japan • CB750 • 1970 • roadster

Indian • USA • Chief • 1948 • roadster

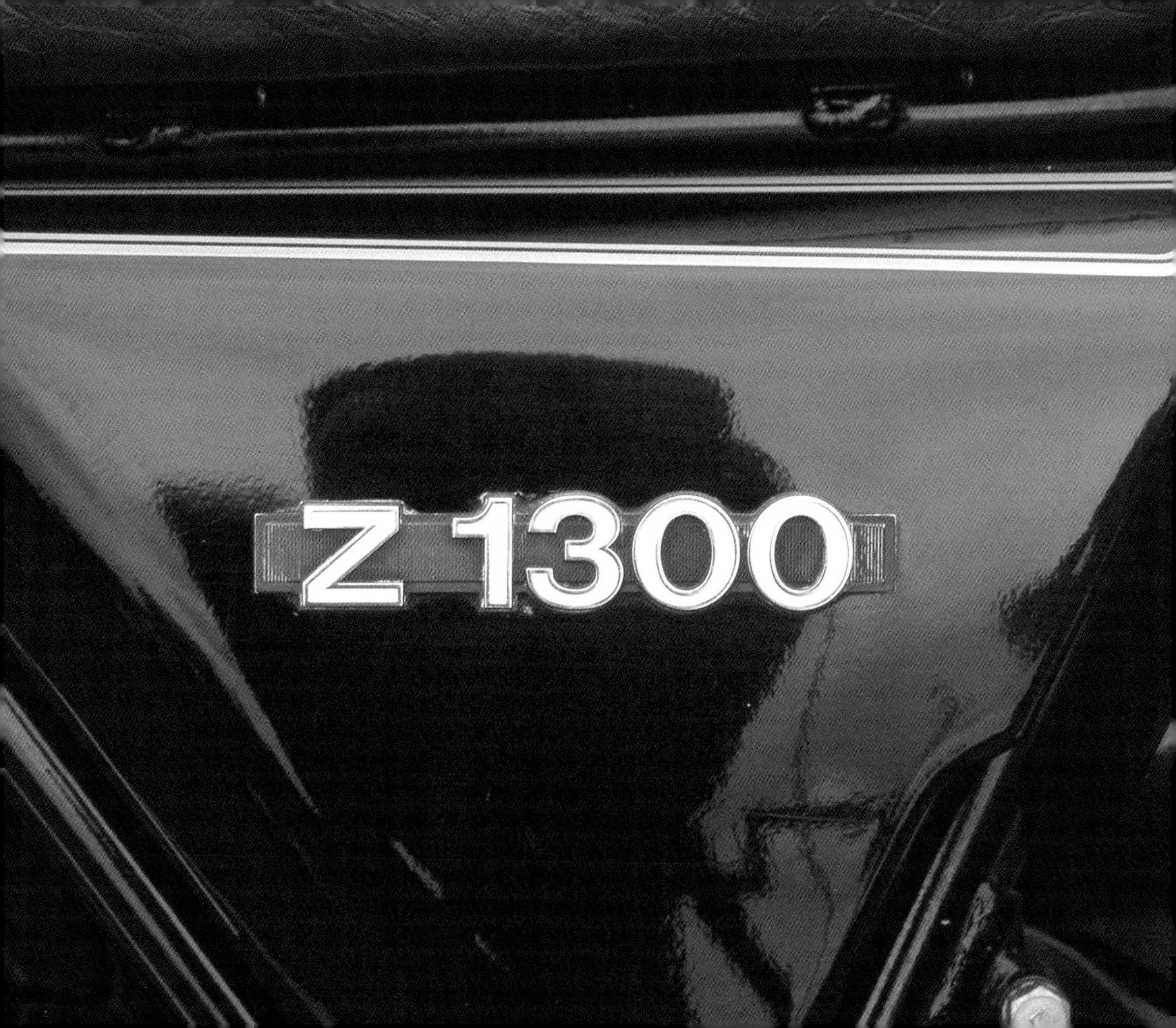
Z 1300

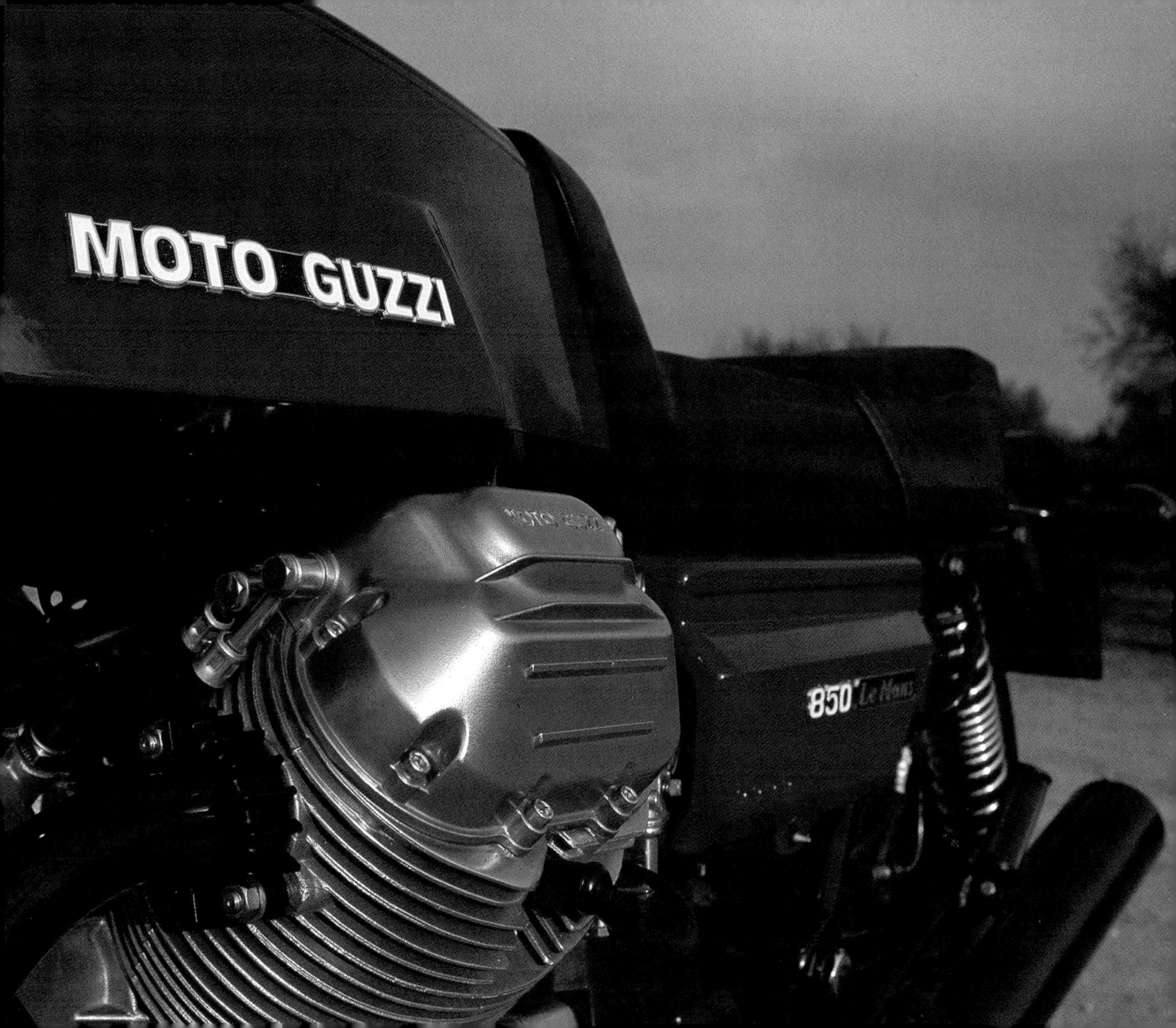
MOTO GUZZI
850 Le Mans

Moto Guzzi • Italy • California • 1980 • tourer

Ner-A-Car • USA/Britain • 1925 • roadster

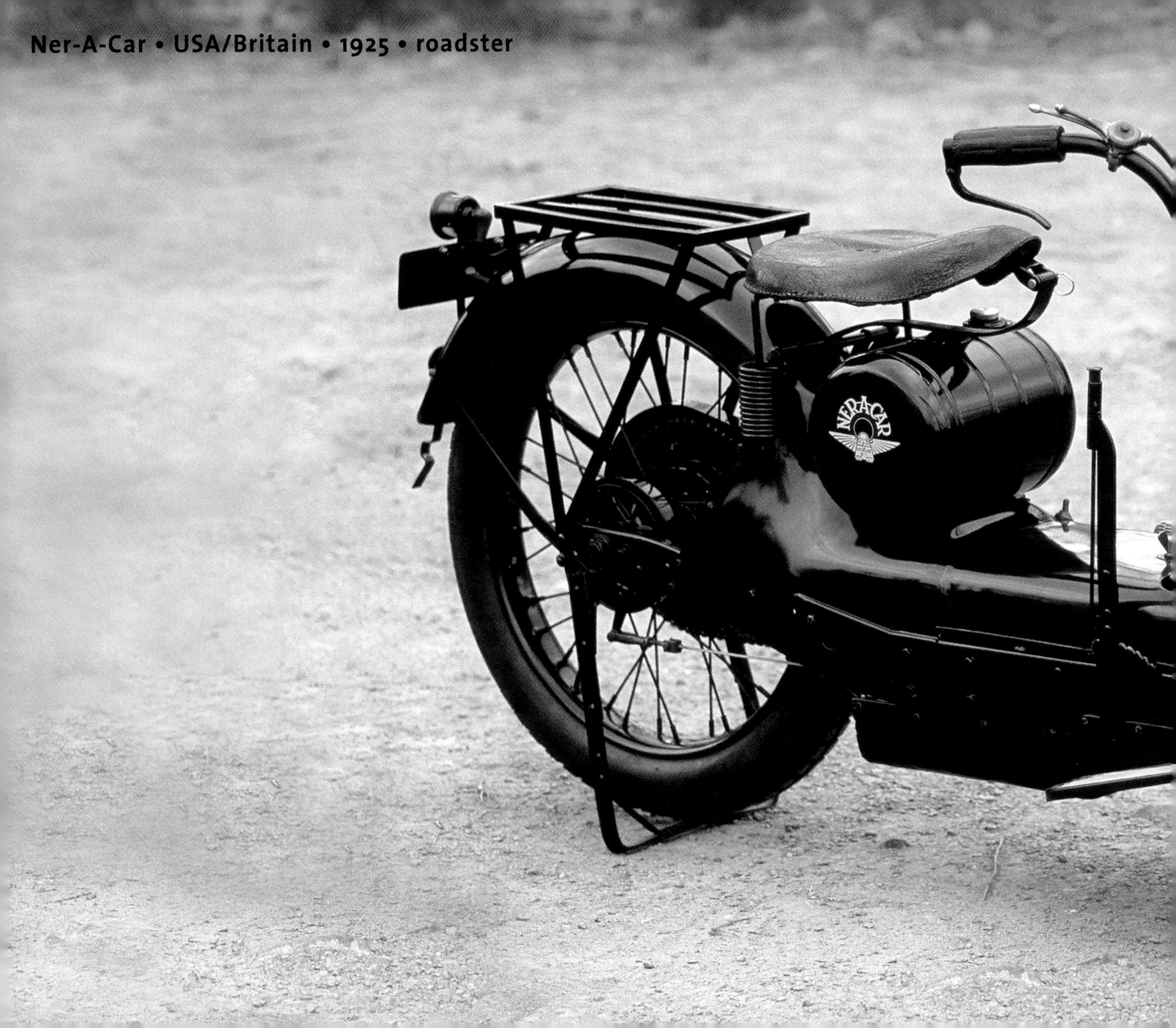

NSU STORTMODELL
BAUJAHR 1927
500 cm   12 PS

Opel • Germany • Motoclub • 1928 • sports

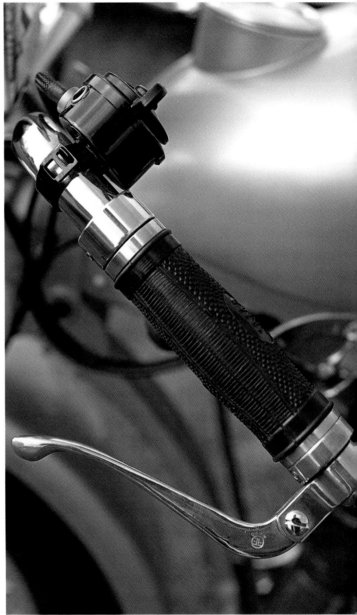

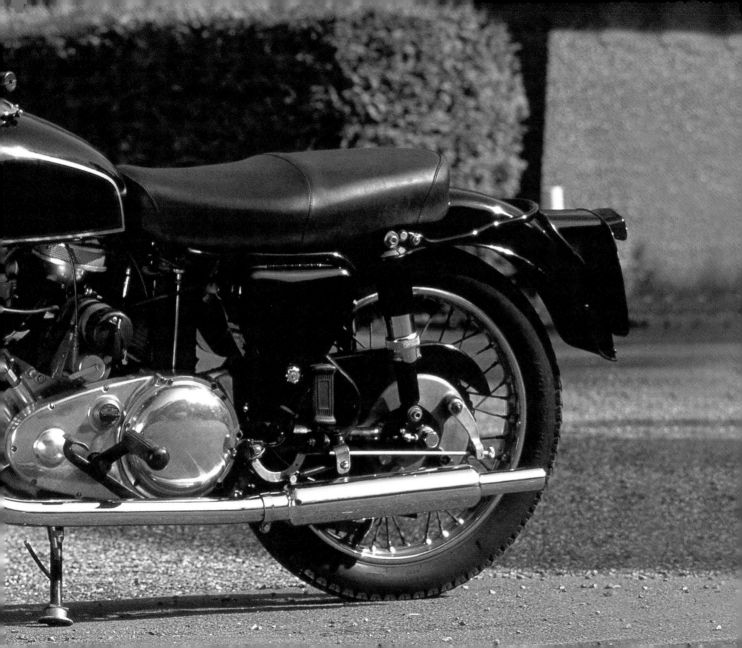

Peugeot • France • 2,25 PS • 1905 • roadster

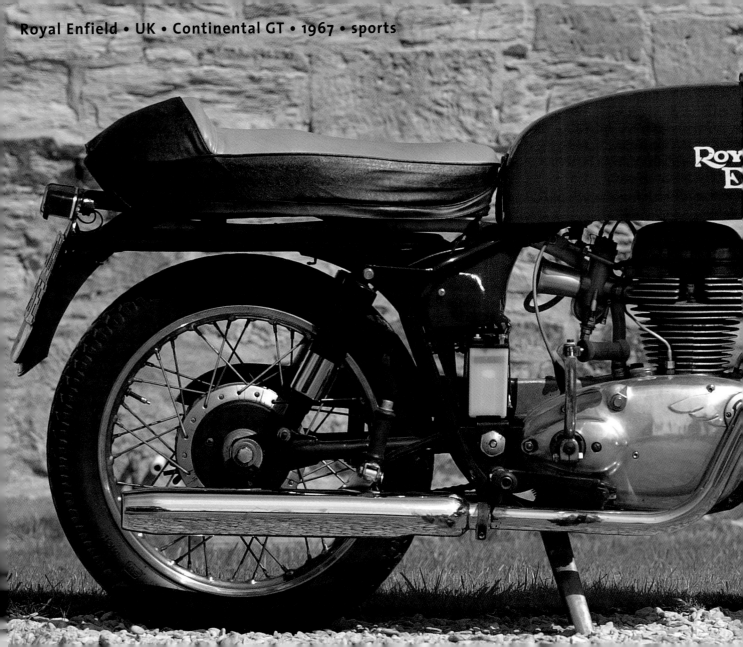

Schüttoff • Germany • 350 ccm • 1923 • roadster

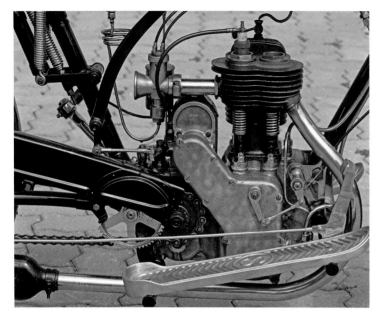

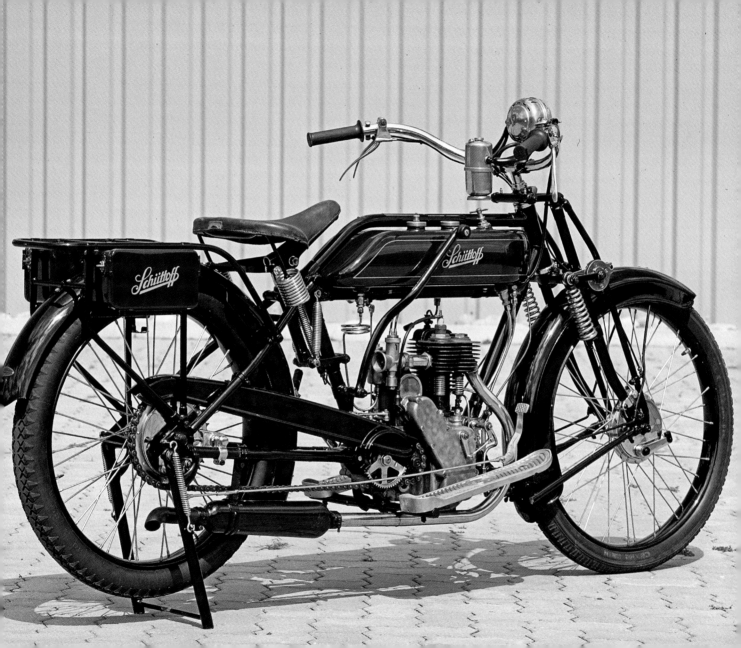

Scott • UK • Flying Squirrel • 1947 • roadster

Standard • Germany • BT350 • 1928 • roadster

Sunbeam • UK • S7 De Luxe • 1949 • roadster

Sunbeam • UK • S8 • 1956 • roadster

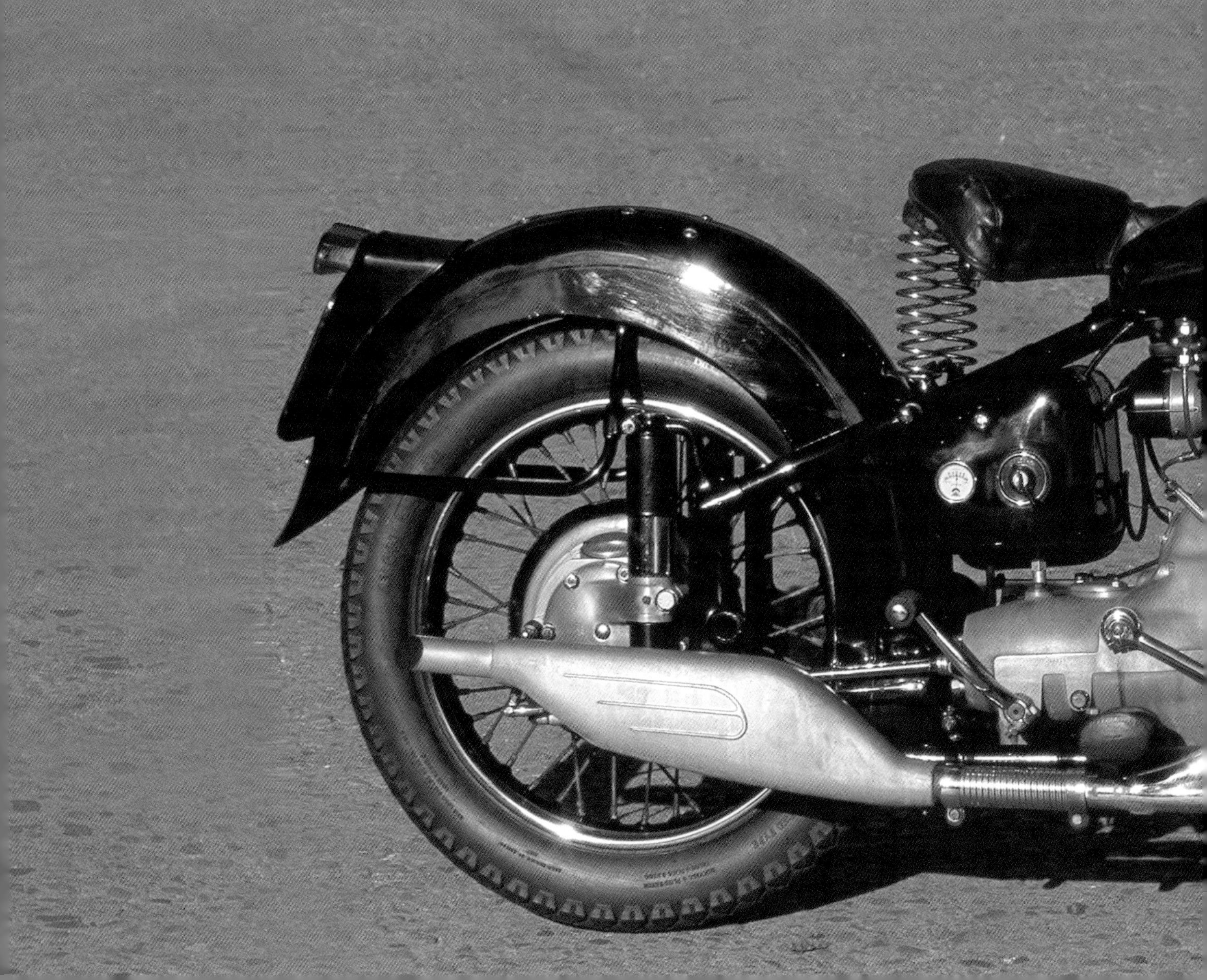

Suzuki • Japan • GSX1300R Hayabusa • 1999 • sports-tourer

Triumph • UK • Speed Twin • 1946 • roadster

MFF 951

Triumph • UK • Daytona 675 • 2005 • sports

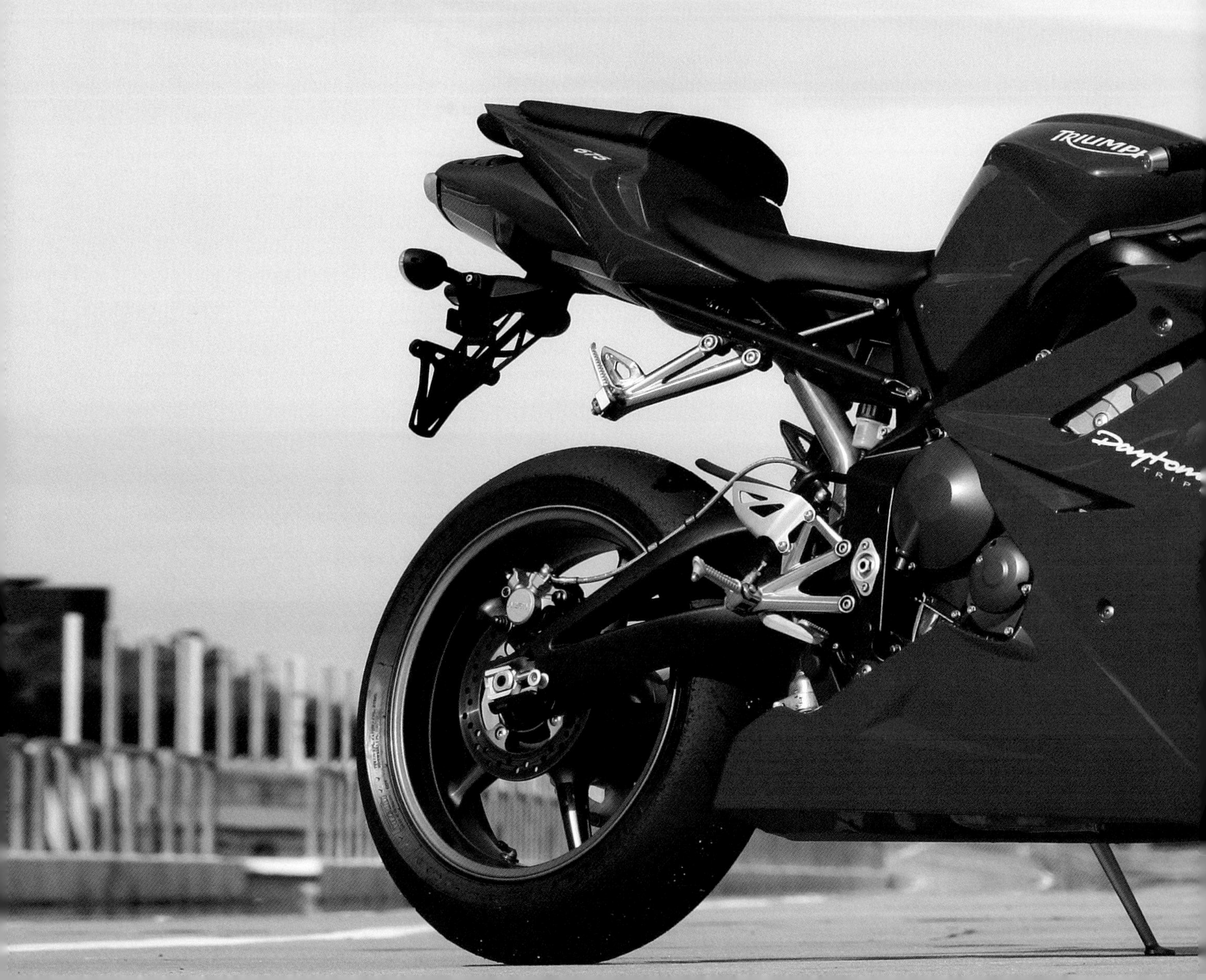

Velocette • UK • LE • 1957 • roadster

XEL 359

Victory • USA • Hammer • 2005 • cruiser

Vincent • UK • Rapide Series C• 1950 • sports

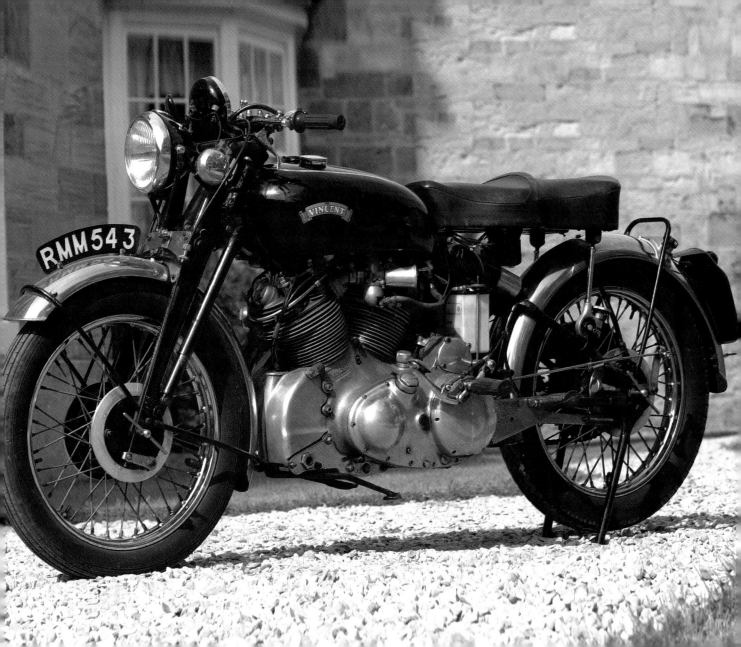

Voxan • France • Café Racer • 2003 • sports

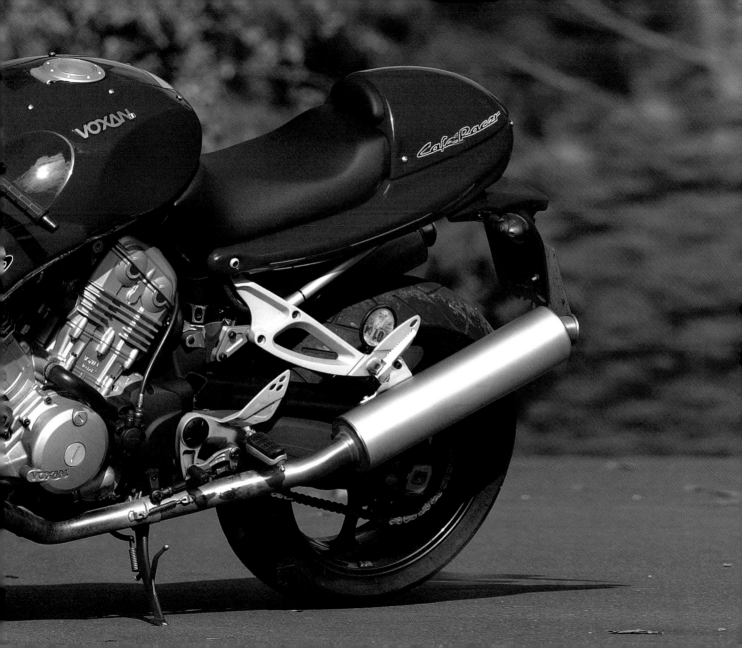

Wanderer • Germany • 2-Zylinder-Modell • 1922 • roadster